THE MESSENGER
the play

adapted by Ross Mueller
from the novel by Markus Zusak

CURRENCY PLAYS

First published in 2008
by Currency Press Pty. Ltd.,
PO Box 2287, Strawberry Hills, NSW, 2012, Australia.
enquiries@currency.com.au
www.currency.com.au
in association with
Canberra Youth Theatre.

NATIONAL LIBRARY OF AUSTRALIA CIP DATA

Author:	Mueller, Ross, 1967–.
Title:	The messenger: the play / Ross Mueller and Markus Zusak.
ISBN:	9780868198477 (pbk.)
Series:	Current theatre series.
Other Authors / Contributors:	Zusak, Markus.
Dewey Number:	A822.4

Typeset by Dean Nottle for Currency Press.
Printed by BookPOD, Melbourne.

Contents

Acknowledgments

Canberra Youth Theatre (CYT) is proudly supported by its members, the ACT Government through artsACT and the ACT Health Promotions Grant Program, and the Australian Government through the Australia Council, its arts funding and advisory body.

The adaptation of *The Messenger* was made possible through the generous support of Paperchain Bookstore and The Rock Development Group whilst the CYT Actors Ensemble is proudly supported by Canberra Milk. CYT would also like to acknowledge the invaluable ongoing support of DesignEdge and 'pling.

This play exists due to the creativity and support of many people including: Markus Zusak, Ross Mueller, Pip Buining, Sharon Casey, Hadley, Caroline Fulton, Mark Gordon, Linda McHugh, Paschal Daantos-Berry, Stephen Barker, Estelle Muspratt, Anthony Arblaster, Anne Marie Serano, QL2 Centre for Youth Dance, Kylie McCaffery, Roger and Maxeme Tall, Maria Efkarpidis, Fiona Inglis, Anthony Blair, Claire Grady, Alex Galeazzi, Kylie Bonaccorso and Ben Sticpewich.

We also extend our thanks to all our friends, families and volunteers who support us in our creative endeavours.

First Production

The Messenger was commissioned and first performed by Canberra Youth Theatre on 24 November 2008 with the following cast:

Markus, The Doorman, Gunman	Tom Heath
Ed Kennedy	Jonathan Sharp
Marv, Man	Joshua Bell
Ritchie	Matthew Paliaga
Audrey	Isobel Nye
Sophie, Misha, Waitress, Henry	Megan Johns
Librarian 1, Police 1, Daryl, Steve, Mrs Boyd, Woman	Tse-Yee Teh
Librarian 2, Police 2, Hannah, Martin, Mr Boyd	Katarina Erceg
Librarian 3, Police 3, Roxanne, Cyrano, Suzanne Boyd	Emily Goodwin
Angelina	Becky Parkinson
Ma	Alison Kelly
Date	Andrew Walker
Giant, Simon	Ensemble

Director / Dramaturg, Pip Buining
Designer, Tobhiyah Feller
Sound Designer, Kimmo Vennonen
Lighting Designer, Mark Gordon
Singer / Songwriter, Andrew Walker

Characters

Markus
The Doorman
Gunman
Ed Kennedy
Marv
Ritchie
Audrey
Sophie
Misha
Henry
Librarian 1
Librarian 2
Librarian 3
Police 1
Police 2
Police 3

Daryl
Hannah
Steve
Martin
Roxanne
Cyrano
Waitress
Mrs Boyd
Mr Boyd
Suzanne Boyd
Woman (Rape Victim)
Man (Rapist)
Angelina
Ma
Date
Giant
Simon (voiced by ensemble)

Pre-records include:
TV voice, Radio voice, Editor voice

Dialogue

The slash / (as indicated) is an interruption point. It provides overlapping dialogue. When used at the end of a sentence the intention is for the next line to come in hard.

Design

Suburban and disaster and biblical. Urban decay can live comfortably with the moral decay in the landscape. Ed is unaware of just how grim his house and neighbourhood have become until he ventures out and sees for himself.

Staging

The ensemble is visible on stage for the entire performance.

Scene One

In the theatre—a streetlight strobes on a suburban disaster.

Powerlines droop and letterboxes are groaning, over-stuffed with catalogues and pizza houses. A lazy clock ticks like a tired typewriter. Decay, detritus, passivity.

A front gate swings. A TV hisses. Talkback mumbles and a tap is dripping. Mosquitoes buzz and the lights come up on MARKUS.

He is sitting on a milk crate holding a yellow folder, listening to the world around him. He begins to tap his pencil.

A Falcon revs, a dog barks, a woman moans, a child cries and somebody is shouting in the distance.

MARKUS begins to write.

An answering machine and MA starts abusing…

Ma I know you can hear me, you lazy little bastard. Now listen. I am baking a cake for Tommy and I need some sugar and flour and eggs. Where did you put the lawnmower, it's never where it's supposed to be and you told me you were gonna bring that bloody coffee table over last week and true to form—my lounge room is vuoto! What am I supposed to do with my coffee cups?! I swear, you are the most useless son on the planet!

Music—a YOUNG MAN plays guitar.

MARKUS writes notes in library books, circling page numbers.

SOPHIE beings to run.

The ENSEMBLE assume their roles in this broken neighbourhood.

A doll's house silhouette of a man and a woman and a child at forty-five Edgar Street, midnight.

AUDREY is kissing SIMON.

A MAN in a balaclava is eating a pie.

MARV is fixing his car.

LIBRARIANS are date stamping books.

RITCHIE is listening to another horse race, with a form guide.

MA sits alone with a telephone in her hand.

ED lies on the couch of his shack, watching Cool Hand Luke *on the TV. He stands up.*

MARKUS stands and there is silence.

Everybody looks to him. Beat and then he speaks…

Markus   I wish I was… I want… Okay… It is abnormally hot for Spring. [*Pause.*] The air conditioner is broken and it is abnormally hot for spring. You know that. I said that. It's hot. We move on. I need an event—we want action. An inciting incident. Like… a bank robbery.

> *Pause and then…*
> *He pulls a stocking over his head, becomes a GUNMAN and screams…*

Gunman   Do what I tell ya and you won't get hurt!

> *Pause.*

Audrey   What do you want us to do?
Gunman   Okay… This is a hold-up! So… get on the floor.
Audrey   Really? The floor?… / That's a little clichéd, don't you think?
Marv   This floor is / disgusting, really. People's feet make me sick.
Ritchie   It's a minefield of disease—I don't want to get infected.
Audrey   Can't we just like—be really, really still or something?
Gunman   No! This is how it starts! Get on the floor. Now!… Please? [*Beat.*] I wanna see some pandemonium!

> *Beat and then pandemonium!—he fumbles with his gun.*
> *ED and AUDREY lie down together. RITCHIE is near the door and MARV is by himself.*
>
> *The rest of the cast become BANK TELLERS and CUSTOMERS— all focussed on the next move.*
>
> *Pause.*
> *LIBRARIAN 1 puts up her hand.*

Yes?

Librarian 1 Is this Scene Twenty-Two?

Gunman What? No. Haven't you been listening?

Librarian 2 Are you sure this isn't Scene Twenty-Two?

Gunman I haven't thought that far ahead yet.

Librarian 3 Then, why are we here?

Gunman I've made a few notes. A few character outlines.

Librarian 1 But this isn't Twenty-Two?

Gunman No. I am definitely starting with a hold-up.

Librarian 2 Very dramatic.

Gunman Thanks. This is it.

Librarian 3 [*to other LIBRARIANS*] I told you. [*To the GUNMAN*] Go ahead. We are prostrate Librarians, ready to be robbed.

Gunman All right. A robbery… yes. [*Pause—then to MISHA*] Hand over all the cash, please… [*reading her name tag*] 'Misha'. That's a nice name.

Misha Thanks. It comes from my mother's side.

Gunman Nice little backstory.

Marv This has got to be the worst bank robbery in history—

Gunman Who's that bastard talking?

Marv It's not me—it's Ed! It's Ed who's talking!

The GUNMAN marches over to the boys on the floor.

Gunman Which one of you is going to be 'Ed'?

Silence.

Do you *want* me to shoot you?!

Ed [*to MARV*] If I get shot—I'm blaming you.

Marv He looks familiar don't you reckon?

Gunman Didn't you / hear what I said?!

Ritchie Just shut your face for once, Marvin!

Gunman [*to RITCHIE*] And what's your name, big mouth?!

Ritchie Big mouth?

Gunman [*turning the gun on RITCHIE*] What do you want?

Ritchie Nothing!… I'm nobody.

Gunman Well shut up, Mr Nobody! This is a bank robbery, not a bloody support group.

Marv [*to the GUNMAN*] Is this going to take much longer?

Gunman What?!

Marv It's about my car.

Audrey Oh my god.

Marv I'm parked in a fifteen minute zone and you're—holding me up.

Gunman So what?

Marv Ironic, I know—but are you going to pay the fine if I get booked?

Gunman Which one's yours?

Marv The light blue Falcon.

Gunman That piece of shit?—I wouldn't piss on it let alone pay a fine on it!

Marv There's no need to be so hostile!

Gunman Hey! This is an inciting incident! I am a gunman! It is my sole purpose to be bloody hostile! /

Marv [*to AUDREY*] Did he say an 'exciting' incident?

Audrey Inciting!

Marv There's a difference?

Audrey Inciting stirs up feelings—it provokes action. Right?

Gunman Action, yeah. That's what this is. Action.

> *Long pause—no action is happening—that's a joke.*

Marv This doesn't feel very inciting to me right / now.

Gunman Right! Hand it over! Gimme the money!

Marv Here we go!

Misha Here's the money!… /

Gunman Okay. Thanks for the—money. [*Beat.*] I'm sorry—if I—you know—traumatised you, Misha.

Misha I'll mention that to my therapist.

Gunman That really is a very pretty name.

Misha That's not her name, that's her job.

Gunman Okay. I have to escape now.

> *The GUNMAN grabs the bag.*

Marv Who is this guy, the Scarlet Pimper-knuckle-head?

Gunman [*to MARV*] Gimme your keys!

Marv What?… No—/ It's an antique. I'm not just giving it away!

Gunman A gunman needs a getaway car—gimme your keys or I'll shoot you!

Ritchie It's a piece of shit, Marv, just give him the keys! Come on!

Marv [*giving the keys*] Please, just be gentle.

Gunman Please, just blow me.

> *The GUNMAN trips over ED. They are face to face and the gun has fallen in front of ED. They both are in reach and there is a pause.*

Do you wanna be a hero?

Ed I've never really thought about it.

> *Beat and ED snatches the gun. The GUNMAN runs. ED runs and then a shotgun blast and a shattering of a windscreen.*
>
> *Commotion.*
>
> *ED walks back into the space—still holding the gun—pause and then...*

This is a lot heavier than I thought it was gonna be.

Markus [*offstage, loud*] Scene Two! Bring in the police!

Scene Two

Three POLICE march straight in with MARKUS and his yellow folder.

Police 1 [*to ED*] Look, son—there's no need to get shirty with me.

Ed Shirty—I quite like that word.

Police 2 Well you can't have it—it belongs to our generation.

Police 3 How did you get the gun?

Ed He dropped it, I picked it up.

Police 1 He dropped the gun? / Oh, how convenient.

Police 2 You expect us to believe that? / And you just picked it up?

Police 3 This is the worst bank robber in history, is he?

Marv He was pretty bad.

Police 1 Who asked you?

Marv Are there some forms I should be filling in?

Police 2 What are you talking about?

Marv Forms... Compensation for the damage to my car. Is there a procedure we should be initiating?

Police 1 Compensation for your car?

Marv Yes. The light blue Falcon.

Police 3 You mean—the light blue shit box?

Marv My car is not a shit box!

All Police Well it's doing a pretty good *impersonation* of a shit box!

> *POLICE burst out laughing, congratulating each other on their joke.*

Marv My car is a victim of crime!

Police 1 [*suddenly serious*] Your car is an absolute outrage! /

Police 2 [*very fierce now*] No indicators—no handbrake—and— /

Marv No windscreen! Yes! I don't need a line-up, officer—I can identify my own car! I need it to get to work and that is why I am asking about the compensation!

Police 3 We should be charging you with driving an un-roadworthy / vehicle!

Police 1 Get yourself into something that is not a danger to the / public!

Police 2 Why don't you 'initiate *that* procedure'?!

All Police Huhu?!

Marv I have my reasons.

Police 1 Like—being a lazy bastard—/

Police 2 —with no bloody money? /

Police 3 —and no bloody prospects?!

Marv Hey! I've got money! I just have other financial priorities.

All Police Safety first, son, every time! [*To ED*] You!... Wait right here.

> *POLICE exit.*
> *MARKUS stays and makes notes.*

Marv There is nothing wrong with the Falcon.

Ed Except the handbrake—the starter motor and the radiator and the indictors / and the front end.

Marv Okay! I need to spend some money on her!

Ed You've got forty grand in the bank and you live with your parents. What 'other financial priorities' have you got, tight-arse?

Marv You might be a hero to some people today—but to me— you're just the dopey prick who put a shotgun blast through my windscreen.

> *POLICE return and MARKUS becomes the GUNMAN in handcuffs.*

6

Ed You're not supposed to bring the offender to confront the victim.

Police 1 You kids today are really hung up on correct procedures, aren't you?

Police 2 Is this the man who held up the bank?

Ed Yes. Absolutely.

Police 3 We need you to be positive.

Marv I don't think you *can be* any more positive than 'Yes, absolutely'!

Ed I'd know this ugly bastard anywhere.

Police 1 You're no oil painting yourself.

Ed No need to get shirty, detective.

Police 2 Thanks for your help, smart-arse.

Ed 'Smart-arse'?

Police 3 That one bridges the generation gap.

All Police [*taking GUNMAN away*] Let's go!

Gunman I'm looking at a dead man.

Ed Dead? / What?

Gunman I won't forget you, Ed Kennedy!

Ed How do you know my name is 'Kennedy'?

Gunman How do I know?

Ed Yeah… how do you know that?

> The GUNMAN starts to laugh and the POLICE drag him away.

How do you know my name?… How do you know my name?!…

> The GUNMAN's laugh bleeds into the next scene.

Scene Three

Recordings and live voices create a chaos.

TV [*voice-over*] The young hero was more surprised by the attention than he was by the fact that he was at the / scene of the crime! He lives in a small shack on the edge of town and works as a cab driver to make a living.

Radio [*voice-over*] … dropped the weapon / while fleeing the scene. Nobody was harmed during the robbery and the money was recovered. Markus Zusak lives in Sydney and watches the same movies over and over again!

Editor The only acknowledgements are—Special thanks to Baycrew, the New South Wales Taxi Council / and to Anna McFarlane for her expertise and commitment. Sex should be like Maths—taught at school and laughed about!

Ensemble 1 / Taxi driver turns hero! Local deadbeat makes good! Taxi driver turns hero! Local deadbeat makes good!

Ensemble 2 He lives alone with a dog called The Doorman! He lives alone with a dog called The Doorman!

ED yells, stopping the chaos.

Ed Okay, that's enough!

The GUNMAN becomes MARKUS again.
Pause.

Markus You can't just stop everything like this.

Ed I just did.

Markus But we've got some momentum going here.

Ed Hey, I'm a hero. I just foiled a bank robbery, I can do anything I want.

Librarian 1 You didn't really *foil* anything.

Librarian 2 He dropped the gun.

Ed I picked it up!

Markus Why?

Ed I dunno—it just happened.

Markus Things don't just happen.

Ed They do to me.

Markus You need direction.

Ed Why?

Markus You drive a cab for a living—a sense of direction is kinda useful.

Ed I drive a cab?

Librarian 3 Why are you so passive?

Ed Hey, I'm a hero. I wasn't scared. It's strange but... most of the time... I don't feel anything.

Markus I think a lot of people feel that.

Ed Do *you*?

Markus Yeah, sometimes.

Ed And what are you going to do about it?

Markus I'm not gonna put my head in an oven, if that's what you mean.

Ed Who are you?

Markus [*a thought occurs*] A few days later.

Ed I don't understand. /

Markus Yes! A few days later Ed Kennedy gets the first message!

Ed A few days later?

Markus Yep.

Ed So, this is going to happen?

Markus Yep.

Ed You are telling me what is going to happen in my future?

Markus Ed. You are going to get a message and you are going to act, and believe me... this first message... it changes everything. If you accept it... it will change everything about your life!

Ed Will my mother stop abusing me on my answering machine?

Markus Spin the wheel and see what happens!

    Beat.

Ed All right. I accept!

Markus Excellent! Okay!—jumping forward a few pages!

    MARKUS becomes THE DOORMAN.

Ed Okay... What are you doing?... Seriously dude, *what* are you doing—people can see you.

Markus I am becoming—The Doorman!

Ed Okay. This is weird now.

Markus I am a seventeen-year-old stinking canine. I previously belonged to your alcoholic father, but since his death... I live with you and I accompany you everywhere.

Ed You live with me?

Doorman Woof.

Ed Where do we live?

Doorman In a suburban disaster. We spend our days—working—eating—sleeping and drinking coffee.

Ed My dog The Doorman drinks coffee?

Doorman And I talk to you.

Ed Oh yeah—that's kinda cool. Why do you drink coffee?

Doorman Because you give it to me! Do you know how bad that is for me? It is going to give me diabetes and liver trouble at the very least.

Ed I'm sorry.

Doorman Don't say it unless you mean it.

Ed I do! I don't want to hurt anybody… do I?

Doorman I dunno—I'm a dog, right?

Ed Why am I driving a cab?

Doorman Because Audrey drives a cab.

Ed Oh… Audrey. She was lying next to me in the robbery. I can still feel her leg touching mine.

Doorman She's a helluva human.

Ed Am I in love with Audrey?

Doorman What do you think?

Ed I think I can still feel her leg touching mine.

Doorman Growl.

Ed Aren't I too young to be driving a cab?

Doorman Pointy ears—I'm a dog—I'm not Doctor Spock. I don't have all the answers.

Ed Who does?

Doorman You.

Ed I don't think so—

Doorman Trust me! The first message arrives one day after the robbery! You go to our normally empty letterbox and—Ta dah!—The message is waiting for you! Woof!

A pause and then a playing card floats gracefully from the sky.

Ed A playing card is the beginning of the rest of my life?

Doorman Aren't you excited?

Ed Not really. I was expecting something a little more—dramatic.

Doorman Hey—there's some handwriting—somebody's written on it! Oh—ahh!… a mystery!

Ed Did you write this?

Doorman Ed, are you trying to be cruel? I don't have any thumbs.

Ed Why is somebody putting a playing card in my letterbox?

Doorman Well, that's a good question! What does it say?

Ed Ace of diamonds. 'Forty-five Edgar Street. Midnight.'

Doorman Sounds like a quest!

Ed What kind of knucklehead sends a playing card to somebody, like this?... Fuck... Of course!

Doorman What?

Ed The Gunman! He knew my name! Maybe he knows where I live.

Doorman I think you're barking up the wrong tree.

Ed Is something bad going to happen to me?!

Doorman What can I tell ya?—I've got a wet nose and I lick myself.

> *Suddenly the phone rings and ED jumps.*
>
> *The DOORMAN becomes MARKUS and directs the transition of the scene.*
>
> *Music.*

Ma [*phone voice-over*] I know you're listening to this and you're too lazy to get off that stinking couch of yours! I wanna know where my coffee table is! You promised me, Ed, you bloody promised me! And if you can't be buggered, fine! I'll hire a bloody professional! You shit me to tears, Ed Kennedy! Don't make promises that you know you cannot keep!

Scene Four

Markus Annoyance! A card game at Ritchie's parents' house. Ed, Audrey, Marv and Ritchie—the four friends are playing. They are getting used to life after the robbery and their old mate—the new hero—Ed! The Doorman is asleep at his master's feet.

> *MARKUS becomes THE DOORMAN.*
>
> *While the dialogue continues, talkback radio kicks in—low and quiet.*

Ritchie Why do you think one of us sent it to you?

Ed Just answer the question.

Marv I don't have the time to come up with something as dumb as this.

Ritchie Exactly. Marv's too busy to be dumb.

Audrey Is it you?

Ritchie No. I'm too lazy.

Audrey So, you have the time—

Ritchie But I lack a motive. For anything really—I am motive-less.

Ed [*to MARV*] Do you think it was The Gunman?

Audrey What? / Are you serious?

Ritchie The Gunman? / That's not really—likely to happen, is it?

Audrey It's not a crime to send a playing card in the mail.

Ed He knew my name—remember?

Marv I saw your mum in the street. She asked me to give you a message—

Ed What is it?

Marv You're a dickhead.

Ed Fuck off, Marv.

Marv That's what she told me to tell you.

Ed No need to be an arsehole.

Marv You're being a bit of tool, Ed.

Audrey Lotta love in the house tonight, people.

Ed Why does she hate me so much?

Marv Maybe it's because she thinks you're a dickhead.

Ed Piss off. /

Marv Up yours. /

Ed Fuck you. /

Marv Which reminds me—The Annual Sledge Match is coming up. Who's playing?

Ritchie I'm playing.

Marv [*playing with RITCHIE*] Excrement! What about you, Mr Tool?

Ed [*to RITCHIE, referencing the card*] Did you send this ace to me?

Marv Come on, man—I asked you a question.

Ed I need an answer.

Audrey It might have to be me.

Marv Hello?

Ed [*to Audrey*] So you sent it?

Audrey I'm the smartest one here.

Ritchie So modest too.

Marv Sorry—am I wearing my 'invisible suit' again?

Audrey I'm just saying, out of all of us—I am the most likely to think up something this ridiculous.

Ed Turn that shit off… Ritchie? I can't concentrate!

Ritchie No need to get shirty about it.

Marv Speaking of shirts—none will be required for the Sledge Match, bare feet and chests only—wanna get back to nature—keep it green for the team. Will you be putting your hand up, Ed?

Ed Why would somebody put a playing card in my letterbox?

Audrey Forget the ace—it doesn't matter. Read the words... 'Forty-five Edgar Street. Midnight.' Somebody has written this for you.

Marv Edgar Street?

Ed Yeah—I know.

Audrey Somebody wants you to go there.

Ed Why?

Audrey Because the world is bigger than Ritchie's kitchen.

Ritchie Clearly, you have been chosen, Ed.

Ed What am I gonna do in Edgar Street—it's such a shit hole.

Marv It's not that bad.

Ed If Edgar street was a car it would be a light blue Falcon.

Marv / Just—play cards, come on. Deal.

AUDREY begins to deal the cards.

Ed It would have a busted muffler and a yellow canary / slapped on it!

Marv We are here / to play Annoyance, Ed!

Ed Nothing good could ever happen at midnight on Edgar Street.

Marv How the fuck would you know?! You've never even been there!

Ed Because it's a bloody shit hole, Marv!

Marv Why don't you just shut your mouth for once?

Ed Why are you so shirty all of a sudden?

Ritchie Suzanne used to live on Edgar Street.

Ed Who?

Audrey Suzanne Boyd.

Ed I didn't know that.

Audrey Yes, you did.

Ed I forgot.

Marv You forgot about Suzanne?

Ed She was like—a lifetime ago.

Marv Try three years, mate.

Ed Marv... come on. It wasn't like she was your girlfriend, was she?

Ritchie Jesus—Ed. /

Ed He hasn't seen her in three / years.

Marv Being a hero has changed you, hasn't it?

Ed I haven't changed.

Marv I think you have.

Ed Marv, I haven't even changed my socks! Suzanne—left. Maybe it just wasn't meant to be, old buddy. If I have offended you... I am sorry.

Marv *If* you have offended / me?

Ed Gimme a break—let's play cards.

Marv Ed. Wait, wait... You've got something on your face—oh, it's your outrageous prejudice! Your head is so far up your own arse you think the whole world is shit! Deal me out, Audrey.

Ed So you're leaving?

Marv I've gotta work tomorrow. I need the money.

Ed You've got forty grand in the bank!

Marv Jesus! Why do you tell the whole world about my life?!

Ed Okay! Look—I might have said the wrong thing about Suzie!

Marv You *might* have said / the wrong thing?!...

Ed I'm saying that I'm sorry for that now, okay?

Marv How could you possibly say the wrong thing, Ed, when you don't know what the hell you're talking about?

> *MARV exits the scene.*
> *Pause.*

Ritchie Some joker's put an ace of diamonds in your letterbox. Get over it.

Ed Was it you?

Ritchie Are we gonna play Annoyance or what?

Audrey I've had enough.

Ed Audrey...

Audrey I'll see you later, Ritchie.

> *AUDREY stands and leaves.*
> *ED begins to follow her.*

Ritchie Where are you going?

Ed I can't just let her leave—

Ritchie But you *can* just leave me?

Ed Ritchie, gimme a break. I'm sorry.

Ritchie No you're not.

> *ED and THE DOORMAN walk out after AUDREY.*

The three of them stand on the street together.
Long pause.

Scene Five

Doorman So you're just going to stand here?
Ed Shut up.
Audrey Are you talking to me?
Doorman 'Are you talking to me?'... That's from *Taxi Driver*.
Ed What?...
Doorman You both drive cabs—that's funny. [*Beat.*] To me that's funny.
Ed Yes, okay. / I get it—shut up.
Audrey What are you saying?
Ed I said—it's abnormally hot for spring.
Audrey Abnormally?

THE DOORMAN nudges ED closer toward AUDREY.

Ed Yeah.
Audrey What are you doing, Ed?
Ed I have to pick up this coffee table for my mum. I'm late—I promised—she's hounding me. Man... what a woman.
Audrey You were so—out of line in there.
Ed Yep.
Audrey Is it shock?
Ed What shock?
Audrey Are you in shock—because of the robbery?
Ed I don't know. Are you? You were right next to me. That was weird, don't you think? The four of us—all in the bank together when that ugly bastard pulls a gun. Where are you going now?
Audrey Don't— / Please—don't ask me that.
Ed I'm—just—saying—do you wanna come over? Hang on the couch—watch a movie... *Cool Hand Luke*... again? It doesn't have to be this difficult.
Audrey What are you going to do?
Ed I dunno. Go and pick up her coffee table.
Audrey I mean—what are you going to do about Edgar Street?
Ed Put aside my 'prejudice' and find out for myself.

15

Audrey Do you think that's a smart thing to do?

Ed Are you still seeing that guy from work?

Audrey Simon?

Ed That's the one. Are you sleeping with him?

Doorman What?

Audrey What if I am?

Ed Okay.

Audrey 'Okay'…?

Ed I mean—okay—good for you. I'm pleased you're happy. Is it—everything you want it to be?

Audrey It's no strings attached.

Ed Do you think that's a smart thing to do?

Audrey It's what I'm doing, it's my business.

Ed You wanna lift?

> *AUDREY looks at him.*

I'm just saying—I can give you a lift home… if you like?

Audrey I think we're heading in different directions.

> *AUDREY leaves.*
> *There is a pause and then…*

Doorman 'I think we're heading / in different directions'?

Ed Oh, that is so bad, isn't it? That is so bad for us.

Doorman When a girl tells you to be careful—you know you're in trouble. But a closer like—'we are heading in different directions'—she just sunk our battleship.

Ed I'm getting relationship advice from my dog now?

Doorman Hey—I have actually *had* relationships, you know? Why did you ask her about sleeping with Simon?

Ed I was trying to make conversation.

Doorman You really have no idea, do you?

Ed This world is running rings around me.

Doorman That makes you the centre of something pretty gigantic.

Ed Yeah… [*Beat.*] You wanna coffee?

Doorman This late at night?… Yeah—why not?… I know a place. [*He begins walking off.*] A little disaster in the darkness on the edge of town. I can always get a table. Are you coming or what?

Scene Six

THE DOORMAN becomes MARKUS with his notebook.
Music begins.

Markus We hear music and Sophie begins to run!
Sophie [*while running*] Sophie is running in bare feet. She runs
because she loves it and Ed watches her. He sits at first and then
eventually he begins to fall in behind her—he is running also—
she gets faster and he tries to catch up—he cannot. She runs on
and Ed is left panting for breath—This is the beginning of a habit.
Markus Scene Seven...

Scene Seven

Markus One dog barking. A gate. Mosquitoes. Paint flaking. A
Monaro with a busted muffler—TV too loud. This is Edgar Street.
Forty-five. Midnight. One streetlight on one observer. He is
standing across from the house. Nothing happens for a long time
and then—a clock strikes midnight and silence! A big drunk man
comes stumbling home. He yells and goes into the house. He
slams the door and the hallway explodes into an amazing white
light. A silhouette of three people—the man, a woman and a
child, and then darkness. We can hear the ticking again. Angelina
appears on the porch—the next scene begins. Angelina remains
on the porch—throughout the following. Ed is at home.
Ed I hide in their darkness, this scene plays out—the same every
night. It's a horror show on Edgar Street and I... I have been
watching for weeks.
Angelina Have you come to help us?

> *ANGELINA is joined by her MOTHER. They comfort each other*
> *while the scene continues.*

Ed This man is a rapist and I am doing nothing about it.
Markus You are the hero and the hero always refuses the quest at
first but eventually—the unavoidable can no longer be avoided...
I didn't make that up—that is the Human Experience. The hero
becomes entangled for emotional reasons.
Angelina Have you come to help us?!

Markus Our character is defined through action. It's not what we say—it's what we do, that counts.

Angelina Are you going to help us?

Ed [*to MARKUS*] What happened to my father?

Markus He was a delivery man. He died in an armchair.

Angelina Are you going to help us?

Ed I have to take the coffee table to Mum's place.

Markus Her father is raping her mother.

Ed It might—work itself out. He might change…

Markus Why would he change?

Ed I don't know.

> *The sounds of Edgar Street around midnight.*
> *A silhouette of the family inside.*

Markus Are you listening?… Christ, it's deafening… Why can't the world hear?! /

Ed Because it doesn't care.

Markus You have been chosen.

Ed For what?

Markus What do you think?

> *A ticking clock.*
> *The lights fade on both worlds and the next scene begins in darkness.*

Scene Eight

Ma Well, well, well—look what the cat dragged in!

Ed How are you, Ma?

Ma Working my bloody freckle off, as usual!

Ed How's the coffee table goin'?

Ma Go and have a look.

> *Lights up on on Ma's place—ED is looking at the coffee table.*
> *ANGELINA and THE DOORMAN are with him—quiet and close.*

Ed Oi!… This isn't the one I delivered!

Ma [*entering*] I didn't like that one. Not good enough.

Ed I got off work an hour early and now it's not bloody good enough?!

Ma No. That pine one was shit. I was talking to Tommy on the phone and he said pine was ordinary and it wouldn't last.

Ed Talking to bloody Tommy… I bloody knew it! Bloody hell.

Ma Your brother knows about coffee tables, Ed! Believe me! He bought himself a cedar table in the city. Talked the bloke down to three hundred and got the chairs for half price.

Ed So what?

Ma So what?! Tommy knows about furniture! Not like some other people who shall remain nameless, like you!

Ed Why didn't you ask me to bring *this one* over for you?

Ma Why would I do a stupid thing like that for?!

Ed You made me bring you the pine one!

Ma It took you a month to get it here! You'll never be a delivery man!

Ed What's that supposed to mean?

Ma You know what it means!

Ed Why do you hate me?

Ma Don't be ridiculous!

Ed I / I am not—I just want to know—why do you hate me, Ma?

Ma Tommy told me that there was a great deal on these tables and I think that Tommy was right! He wouldn't lie to his mother!

Ed He's not perfect.

Ma He's pretty close compared to you!

Ed You're exasperating! You could drive a man to drink!

> *Pause. They lock eyes.*

Ma I don't want that dog in here stinking up my house.

Ed / This used to be his home!

Doorman This used to be our home.

Ma I never wanted him in the / first place! He is your responsibility!

Ed He lived here for seventeen years, Ma. And now he's not welcome?

Ma That's right! /

Ed Then neither am I.

Ma Oh—don't get all dramatic, for God's sake!

Ed I know where I'm not wanted!

Ma Those are your words, Ed, not mine.

Ed Yeah, and these are my words too… 'This is the crappiest coffee table I have ever seen in my stupid life!'

Scene Nine

ED and ANGELINA exit.

ANGELINA automatically slips her hand into the hand of the adult—which in this case is ED.

Ed You can fill a cathedral with the lost souls in this town... What does salvation look like?

Doorman Depends on who we're tryin' to save.

Angelina Have you called the cops?

> *ED stops. They are still holding hands and SOPHIE runs laps again.*
>
> *They are watching her—she is wearing shoes and the shoes are slowing her.*
>
> *SOPHIE trots past again—like wiping the frame in a film.*

Ed Sophie is running. She's better in bare feet. She should chuck those shoes away.

Doorman Why don't you tell her?

Ed Me?

Doorman Sometimes we know things—but we need to hear them from somebody else—somebody who cares.

> *ED begins to follow SOPHIE.*
> *MARKUS becomes THE DOORMAN.*

Ed Excuse me—

> *She ignores him.*

Excuse me... Sophie.

> *She stops.*

Sophie Get away form me, pervert! I know what you're doing!

Ed Really? What am I doing?

Sophie You're following me!

Ed No, I'm not—

Doorman Yes, you are.

> *A moment—obviously he is following her.*

Ed Okay—but not like a weirdo.

Sophie You sit in the bushes and watch me! I've seen you—that is weird.

Ed I don't do that.

Doorman Yes you did.

Ed Okay, I did. But I'm sorry.

Sophie I'm gonna call the cops.

Ed Shit, why does everybody wanna call the cops / today!

Sophie Don't swear at me—my dad knows karate!

Ed Listen—I just wanna ask you a question...

Sophie What is it? 'Can I jerk off in the bushes while I watch you running?'

Ed No, nothing like that...

Sophie Well—what is it?

> *Beat.*

Ed Why are you wearing shoes?

Sophie Because that's what normal people do... Isn't it?

Ed Yeah—but... I don't think they're helping you.

Sophie If I'm going to win ... I need these shoes. My dad gave them to me.

Ed I've seen you run... They're slowing you down.

> *There is a moment between them. Then action!*
> *ED hunts through the detritus on the stage. He finds a box about the size of a shoebox and dusts it off. He presents it to SOPHIE.*

I think you will win in these.

> *She opens the box—it is empty. She looks to him.*

Sophie Who are you?

Ed Ed... I'm Ed Kennedy.

Sophie Am I imagining you?...

Ed No. I'm just another stupid human.

Sophie How do you know my name, Ed?

Ed I don't know—but I do.

Sophie Yeah, you did.

> *She wanders away.*

Doorman The unavoidable is confronted.

Ed And it didn't hurt a bit.

> *Music.*
>
> *ANGELINA stays with SOPHIE. SOPHIE takes off her shoes and she stretches her toes. ANGELINA throws her own shoes away. SOPHIE doesn't see ANGELINA. They both yell with joy and excitement and they run around the space.*
>
> *They continue to run into the darkness when we hear the sounds of Edgar Street.*

Scene Ten

A silhouette of three people—the man (RAPIST), the WOMAN and ANGELINA—and then darkness.

The lights fade.

ANGELINA leaves the silhouette—she accompanies ED into the next scene.

Scene Eleven

THE DOORMAN is drinking coffee and ED is looking at the playing card.

ANGELINA wanders in and starts stroking THE DOORMAN.

ED sees this and is unsure how to respond. He starts to look for distractions—rearranging photographs, etcetera.

Angelina When are you going to save us?

> *ED hears this but does not respond.*

When are you coming to save us, Ed? [*Pause.*] Why are you ignoring me?

> *ED starts pulling the place apart, cleaning and moving things.*
>
> *He finds a picture of his family. He turns and sees SOPHIE and the WOMAN and the CHILD. They all smile at him—they are with THE DOORMAN.*
>
> *ED turns on the vacuum cleaner and tries to block it out of his system.*

Why are you ignoring us?... When will you stop ignoring us?!

ED smashes the vacuum cleaner off fast.

Ed Bad things happen to good people! None of this is my fault! It's not!

He holds the playing card to ANGELINA.

Go home... You live here! I saw you once—now let me go.

Angelina I'm part of you.

Ed No you're not—

Angelina Yes I am... You can't forget me.

Ed I—don't—know—what—to—do.

Angelina Yes you do. [*Pause.*] Yes—you—will.

She beckons him to follow her.
He is drawn to her but when he gets to a certain point, he cannot continue to move.

So many souls inhabit this earth. And no matter how lost or dead we feel inside—we all hope somebody will remember us. Somebody will empathise.

THE DOORMAN rests a paw on ED.

ANGELINA, her MOTHER and SOPHIE lie down with THE DOORMAN.

MARV enters and watches the scene. Then...

Marv Everybody's waiting. [*Pause.*] Ed? Don't you wanna play Annoyance?...

Throughout the following THE DOORMAN becomes MARKUS and ED begins to dismantle the vacuum cleaner—and assembles a reasonable replica of a sawn-off shotgun.

What about Audrey? Is she gonna play?

Ed Why ask me?

Marv You two are always together—

Ed Go and ask Simon.

Marv But you're coming, right?... It's card night.

Ed Marv... I just can't make it. I've got a heap on my plate right now.

Marv Yeah—I can see that.

Ed What time is it?

Marv I dunno... Eleven thirty or somethin'. We're sitting there like morons and you're Doris Day—cleaning up this shit hole. It's like dusting in a coalmine. I'm in no mood for your litany of crap today, Ed. Just get over to Ritchie's and play some cards or I won't let you play in the annual sledge match this year? What the fuck are you doing?!

Ed [*holding the gun up at MARV*] Marv. I have to kill somebody tonight.

Marv Okay... Will you swing by, later on?

> *Beat and then...*
>
> *Music.*
>
> *ED grabs a bottle of vodka and shoves the gun into the back of his pants.*

Markus Scene Twelve. Ed and The Doorman are on Edgar Street. Waiting for a rapist to arrive.

Scene Twelve

The clock strikes twelve.

ED and THE DOORMAN are on Edgar Street.

The RAPIST arrives and, while the music is playing, ED stops him.

Rapist You're in my way.

> *ED offers the RAPIST a bottle of vodka.*
>
> *The RAPIST grabs it and drinks from it.*
>
> *The RAPIST takes another long drink and ED rushes him— holding the back of the RAPIST's head, ED forces the vodka down into his throat.*
>
> *He is almost drowning the man and then he knocks him off his feet.*
>
> *They fall to the ground, covered in alcohol and spluttering.*
>
> *ED pushes the RAPIST face down onto the ground. He sticks his knees into the man's back and holds the gun into the back of his head.*

Ed I've seen you.

Rapist I don't know what you're talking about.

Ed I know you hurt her! You live for her humiliation! A man like you, deserves to die!

Rapist Okay! I'm sorry... I'll stop.

Ed Stop what?

Rapist I will stop raping her.

Ed How can I trust you?

Rapist Believe me.

Ed No. Not good enough... I'll give you one more chance to convince me, but if you don't—I'm gonna shoot you in the back of the head. Now!... How can I be sure that you are going to stop?!

Rapist Because change is more important than revenge. [*Beat.*] You're torturing me—because this is what I do to her... right? I agree with you. I am a vile character. I said I'm sorry—I will change... Is that the right answer?

> *Pause.*
>
> *ED almost collapses.*
>
> *THE DOORMAN grabs him and helps him to his feet.*
>
> *ED drops the gun and looks at THE DOORMAN, before walking from the stage.*
>
> *THE DOORMAN becomes MARKUS.*

Markus On your feet.

> *The RAPIST stands.*

Don't say anything. Just—disappear.

Rapist Don't you like me anymore?

Markus I wanted him to kill you.

Rapist Killing me murders any goodness in you. [*Pause.*] I know what I am.

Markus You are a secondary character!

Rapist I am a powerful force!

> *MARKUS hits the RAPIST with the gun and they fight viciously— evil—and animalistic.*

Eventually the RAPIST is stronger and holds MARKUS by the throat.

What do you want from me, Markus?

Markus I want you to disappear!

Rapist Too late! I am alive! Created!

Throughout the following monologue the ENSEMBLE whisper underscoring echoes of the monologue. They challenge MARKUS with their presence.

Nameless and disgusting—a filthy drunken rapist—an irredeemable man! You brought me here for a purpose—I am a single moment in another man's story and now you want me to change because a gun is at my head? No. I was imagined and so I exist. My stinking actions are imprinted on the memory of this page. Those who can see me—will not forget me. I will spend every night in bed with you and you and you and you and you. Because of you. I am the worst of human experience and I refuse to vanish simply because you don't want to use me anymore. Every page is infected by my actions—but they are your thoughts. Take responsibility for all your children, not just the ones you think you love. What if it finishes now?... What if I am the last character you ever imagine?... Evil. Imagine that. Lights out.

Lights out.

In the darkness furious music begins.

Scene Thirteen

The music continues.

Lights up fast on a man in a balaclava (DARYL) eating a pie and sauce. He sits at the table in Ed's place.

ED walks in and focuses on the balaclava man at the table.

He realises he needs to find something to defend himself with.

Then another two balaclava figures walk in behind him (HANNAH and ROXANNE) and they whack ED—who falls to the floor.

MARKUS watches while ED is carried into a chair.

They start to slap ED to wake him up. The slaps are slow and gentle at first. Then, of course, they accelerate.

DARYL delivers an almost knockout blow and ED wakes up groggy.

Ed Who sent you?

Daryl We don't know.

Hannah We just do the job and get paid.

Ed No-one pays me.

Daryl No need to get shirty.

Roxanne Can we just get this over with so I can take this bloody mask off?

Daryl Discipline, Roxie, all good hit people have discipline. Now— stand up.

> *ED stands.*
> *DARYL produces a new playing card.*

We know you haven't killed no-one.

Hannah That's a tremendous moral choice.

Daryl So... this is for you.

Roxanne Good luck.

Ed Is this the next message?

Hannah What is this? A rehearsal?

Roxanne Do we have to spell it out?

Daryl Haven't you read the directions?

Roxanne This is the next ace in the pack!

> *She slaps the card onto his forehead.*

Daryl Good luck.

Hannah He's gonna need it... [*To ED*] Get the message?

> *DARYL punches ED in the ribs and ED hits the floor.*
>
> *Music comes back up loud and fast—they pummel him some more.*
>
> *DARYL lays an envelope on the back of ED's neck with the card.*
>
> *The three hit people exit.*
>
> *MARKUS makes sure that ED is still breathing.*
>
> *Then ED finds the next card.*

Ed Ace of clubs. 'You're heading in the right direction.' This is the right direction?...

Music plays.

ED leaves the shack and THE DOORMAN follows him.

ED collapses at Audrey's front door.

A door bell.

AUDREY appears and the music stops.

THE DOORMAN is still with him and ED is holding the envelope.

Scene Fourteen

Audrey God—what happened?
Ed Don't worry about me... Can I come in?
Ensemble [*as SIMON*] Who is it, babe?
Audrey [*turning to the sound of the voice*] Oh... it's just Ed.
Ed 'Just Ed'?
Audrey Will you be home later?—I'll come over later tonight.
Ensemble [*as SIMON*] Are you gonna be out there much longer, babe?
Audrey I won't be long.
Ensemble [*as SIMON*] Missing you already, babe.
Ed I can smell sex on you.
Audrey You know how to make a girl feel special.
Ed Audrey—
Audrey What do you want, Ed?

ED hands her the letter.

[*Reading the letter*] 'Dear Ed. I know what happened on Edgar Street—well done! Now new challenges await. Good luck and keep on delivering. I'm quite sure you realise now that your very life depends upon it.' [*Pause.*] What happened on Edgar Street?
Ed I was sent there to kill a rapist.
Ensemble [*as SIMON*] Who is it, babe?
Audrey Did you kill him?
Ensemble [*as SIMON*] I miss you, babe?
Ed No! I didn't kill him—God.

Audrey 'Your life depends upon it'...? What is going on?!

> *ED grabs AUDREY's face.*

Ed It is abnormally hot for spring... and... I wish I didn't stop that robbery. I wish we could be in love for just one scene. I wish my lips were being hunted by yours. I am... stupidity... in its purest form.

Audrey No... you're not.

Ed Well, what am I?

Audrey You're my best friend.

> *Pause.*

Ed Sometimes...

Audrey What?...

Ed Sometimes I wish I was a dog.

Markus A gentle atmosphere.

> *The ENSEMBLE, ED and THE DOORMAN walk away from AUDREY.*

Ed and The Doorman need to sleep.

Scene Fifteen

Music—a gentle atmosphere.

ED and THE DOORMAN are snoozing.

Playing cards fall gently from the sky—like snow. They cover the stage and the scene is one of peace and beauty.

This moment lasts for a long time.

The music concludes then the LIBRARIANS appear.

Librarian 1 Sylvia Plath and Markus Zusak!

Ed / What the hell?

Librarian 2 No that's not right. It's Morris West.

Ed Are you talking to me?

Librarian 3 Taxi driver, right.

Ed Yes I am.

Doorman You see, to me—that is funny. Because you are and yes it is. [*Beat.*] Oh, it doesn't / matter.

Librarian 1 Is this Twenty-Two?

Ed I don't know how to answer that question.

A banging on the door.

Marv Ed?… Ed? Can you hear me?!

Librarian 1 He doesn't look anything like Sylvia Plath.

Librarian 2 How can you tell?

Librarian 3 He hasn't got his head in an oven.

Doorman He isn't even close.

Marv What's going on, man?

Librarian 2 I told you! We're way too early again, you never listen to me!

Librarian 1 There's no need to get so shirty about it!

Librarian 3 We are librarians! We shall return!

The LIBRARIANS disappear just as MARV bursts into Ed's place. He is dressed for the rugby.

Ed You just broke my door.

Marv Yeah. How about that? Just like a movie… Hey—you're not supposed to bleed from the head like that.

Ed Am I bleeding?

Marv Someone got you good—

Ed The world's going crazy, Marv.

Marv Will you be right to play this afternoon?

Ed Play what?

Marv The Sledge Match.

Ed Yes. I'm right. I'll play. It'll be good for me.

Marv Are you sure?

Ed You think 'Yes. I'm right. I'll play' sounded too ambiguous?

Marv You look like shit.

Ed Marv. I relish the idea of being beaten to a pulp.

Marv Well come on, Mr Fight Club. We've got a game to win.

Scene Sixteen

They walk to the football ground. ANGELINA and SOPHIE and THE DOORMAN accompany them.

A soundscape kicks in:

'What we've got here is failure to communicate.'

A dripping tap somewhere and swinging gate.

Talkback radio.

An intermittent female moan of pleasure and mosquitoes and one young man with a Monaro and a muffler and the following pre-recorded dialogue...

Angelina   There are so many souls that / inhabit this earth.
Rapist   Those who have seen me—will not / forget me.
Marv   This has got to be the worst bank robbery in history—
Ed   Shut up. /
Rapist   I served this plot... I walk this earth.
Gunman   Who's that bastard talking?!
Marv   It's Ed, sir—it's Ed who's talking!
Mr Boyd   Take responsibility for all your / children!
Marv   This gunman is bloody useless.
Ma   I need flour and sugar and eggs, I'm making a cake for your brother.
Gunman   I'll come over there and shoot you!
Markus   You need direction.
Ma   Nothing is ever where it's supposed to be.
Librarian 2   Why don't we just skip forward a few pages?
Librarian 1   What are going to learn from that? / Skipping forward.
Librarian 3   Well, what's he going to learn from playing rugby?
Librarian 2   Don't jump ahead—it'll spoil the ending.

> *ED speaks.*

Ed   Okay! That's it! That's enough!

Scene Seventeen

ED ties THE DOORMAN to a tree.

Doorman   What are you doing?
Ed   Everybody else in the world knows everything about my life.
Doorman   Don't tie me up—don't / abandon me, like this!
Ed   I didn't wanna be hero! I'm not a bloody mind-reader... all right? I'm Ed. I am a suburban bloke! I drive taxis and I just wanna hang out with my mates!... There is nothing wrong with that! All right?!... Just... leave me the fuck alone.

ED joins the team in a tight huddle—both teams are drinking beers—both teams are wearing bare feet. HENRY is their captain and he is making sure the team is stretching and warming up.

Scene Eighteen

Ritchie Christ, you look like shit.
Ed Good to see you too, Ritchie.
Ritchie What happened?
Ed I don't know yet.

> *A GIANT of a man—ED's opposite number—is stretching.*

Henry [*to ED*] That one's yours, that's what you're marking. Don't let him out of your sight.
Ritchie I don't think that's possible.
Henry You should see his big brother.
Ed [*offering his hand*] Good luck.
Giant I'm going to rip your bloody head off.
Ed Is that going to be my ending?
Giant What are you talking about smart-arse?
Ed Smart-arse?
Ritchie Bridges the generations.
Henry Right—*in here!*

> *The team gathers.*

Right—when we get *out there*—what are we going to do to them?

> *Silence.*

Well?...
Ritchie What do you want us to say?
Henry Let's get out there and smash some heads!

> *Wild music—the team roars and runs to position.*
> *ED and the GIANT are face to face.*
> *The game begins—ED is flattened—run after run.*
> *ED continues to run and get beaten to a pulp by the GIANT.*

The ref's whistle is heard and it's half-time.

Okay—okay—half time—rehydrate—everybody grab a beer!
What the hell is going on?... There's only one of youse blokes
havin' a decent crack out there and it's not bloody you or you or
you or you!

Ritchie Who is it?

Henry [*pointing at ED*] Him!

Ed Me?

Marv Him!

Henry This bloke's a deadset legend! What's your name, pal?

Ed My name?...

Henry No—your bloody dog, what do you reckon?

Marv His dog's called The Doorman.

Henry Shut up, you dopey drongo!

Marv No need to get shirty, Henry.

Ritchie It's—Ed—his name's Ed Kennedy.

Henry Well, Ed Kennedy is a superhero compared to you bunch of
fruits! Now come on! Lift your game and show me something,
you drunken, drongo, dopey—dickheads!... Oh! I love ya's all!

ED walks to THE DOORMAN—they just stare at each other.

Marv [*arriving*] Oi—superhero... You still haven't hit that big
bastard yet.

Ed Look at him, Marv—he's bigger than Britney.

Marv [*exiting*] I need more beer if I'm gonna keep running this fast.

Doorman You tied me to a tree!

Ed So what?!

Doorman Don't you want me anymore?

Ed I don't know what's going on.

Doorman You can hear me—you can see me.

Ed But I don't feel a thing.

The GIANT is walking past.

Hey! Next time you get the ball, run at me like your life depends
on it.

Giant You're crazy.

Ed Are you scared of me or something?

Giant Scared of you?

ED kisses the GIANT and the GIANT leaves in a fury.

Doorman That was a very stupid act—
Ed An inciting incident—
Doorman I don't know what that means.
Ed What's it like to be dead?
Doorman Why are you asking me?
Ed I think you might have the answer.

> *Ref's whistle—THE DOORMAN becomes MARKUS.*
> *The players retake the field.*
>
> *Music again and the action begins.*
>
> *The GIANT gets the ball and runs at ED. ED lines him up—there is a huge collision and the music stops. The GIANT has hit the deck.*
>
> *Silence.*

Marv Is he alive?
Henry Who gives a shit?... That's the best Don't Argue I have ever witnessed!

> *ED vomits. He turns to AUDREY.*

Ed I'm alive...
Audrey Only *just.*
Ed I can feel every cell in my body.

> *There is a moment of connection between them.*

The Doorman—where is he?

> *A playing card lies next to the tree.*

Where's my dog?... Where is he?...

> *ED and AUDREY search and ED returns to the playing card. MARKUS watches him pick it up. It is clear that ED is distressed.*

Audrey You haven't done anything wrong, Ed. He'll show up.
Ed What if he doesn't? What if he's gone?... Audrey?... I love him.

> *MARKUS hears this and decides to reanimate THE DOORMAN again.*

34

ED sees him coming and runs up and embraces him.

I'm so sorry. I'm / so sorry. I'm so sorry.

Doorman It's all right. It's going to be all right.

Ed I should never have left you.

Doorman Don't worry—

Ed I know how you feel.

Doorman How do I feel?

Ed Nobody wants to be abandoned...

Doorman Forgive yourself, Ed. [*Pause.*] You got another card?

Audrey What is it?...

ED looks up to AUDREY.

What card is it?

Ed [*checking the card*] Ace of spades.

Audrey Is anything written on it?

Beat.

Ed Will you go to the victory party with me tonight?

Audrey Is that really what it says?

Ed That is really what I'm asking.

Audrey You killed the giant. You won the battle. Go and be the hero tonight.

AUDREY has vanished. ED and THE DOORMAN are alone.

Doorman What does it say?

Ed [*reading*] 'Morris West and Sylvia Plath.' This is it, Doorman... I'm getting close to the end.

Music.

Scene Nineteen

Another phone message while...
ED and THE DOORMAN walk back to his house.
They pass through a human traffic:
A GIRL on a swing and a MAN in a balaclava.
The RAPIST and ANGELINA.
SOPHIE is still running.

ED sees a tired WOMAN and gives her an ice-cream—she is surprised and pleased. She watches as he wanders home.

Ma [*voice-over*] I don't know why I bother to even waste my breath on you. You don't listen and you don't show up and you're just bloody useless and those are your good points. I need somebody to clean out my gutters before the sun crashes into the moon! Scene Twenty!

Scene Twenty

ED and THE DOORMAN arrive to find RITCHIE waiting at Ed's place.

Ritchie Hey—Mr Giant Killer.

Ed What are you doing here?

Ritchie Nothin'... You know me, Ed—that's what I do every day.

Ed You're not going to the party?

Ritchie Nah...

Ed Why not?

Ritchie Why aren't you going?

Ed I dunno.

Ritchie You waiting for Audrey?

Ed No—she's with Simon for sure.

Ritchie Right.

Ed What are you doing here, Ritch?

Ritchie I just wanted you to know that—I'm sorry we've had a bit of a... You know?

Ed Yeah, yeah, I know.

Ritchie I don't wanna—make it so we're... You know?

Doorman Weird?

Ritchie Yeah. [*Pause.*] Did you just say weird?

Ed Yep.

Ritchie That's what I thought—but your lips didn't move.

Ed You're probably just... concussed from the game or something.

Ritchie You're the one who took the big hit. It was courageous.

Ed Was it?

Ritchie Yeah. I was proud it was one of us... I was proud of you.

  Pause.

Ed You wanna beer or somethin'?

Ritchie Um... Yeah—no—I got my bike—Oh... I don't know— What do you reckon? I don't... Ever since that bank thing... You know?... It was really... [*Pause.*] Good game, mate.

Ed You too.

Ritchie Nah... I was just makin' up the numbers. [*Pause.*] Well—I'm gonna—go to the party—you wanna go together?

Ed Um... I was just going to chill out here.

Ritchie That's cool.

Ed You can hang around if you want.

Ritchie No... I might see ya later.

Ed Okay.

Ritchie Cool.

>   *Pause.*

Ed Thanks for dropping in.

Ritchie No worries.

Ed How long were you waiting for me?

Ritchie I dunno. Time speeds up, slows down... The footpath moves—I'm just standing still—I'm happy and sad and furious and forgotten... What's that about?

Ed Sounds like love.

Ritchie Does it? [*Pause.*] I'll see ya later.

>   *RITCHIE exits.*
>   *THE DOORMAN becomes MARKUS.*

Markus Little bits and pieces of us are left inside so many lives. You're walking with Ritchie. You're at the party. You're dancing with Audrey, protecting Angelina. You're inspiring Sophie and you're with your father's memory. Thinking about Morris West and dreaming of Sylvia Plath. You're making an effort, Ed... This is the rest of your life.

Scene Twenty-One

Night music at Ed's place—he is asleep on the couch.

Markus This night Ed is dreaming students in a classroom. Dusty and yellow—

Librarian 1 Books are everywhere.

Librarian 2 Words on a board that nobody can read.

Librarian 3 The teacher appears.

Librarian 3 She ignores Ed and teaches the rest of the class.

Markus The bell rings and there is a heavy silence.

Librarian 3 The teacher beckons Ed to follow her. She gets down onto the floor—she looks up at him. She bends down and puts her head in the oven…

Librarian 1 She turns up the gas

Librarian 2 … and begins to kill herself.

Markus Ed struggles to save her—

Librarian 3 But it is too late.

Markus He tries to revive her.

Librarian 3 He cannot.

Markus In this dream—she is dead.

Librarian 3 He is distressed.

Librarian 2 He wakes up…

Markus Alone with The Doorman again.

Librarian 1 Mosquitoes.

Librarian 2 A buzzing fridge.

Librarian 3 And Sylvia Plath in his head.

Librarian 2 She killed herself.

Librarian 1 Yes.

Librarian 3 Some writers do that, don't they?

Markus I… [*pause*] … become The Doorman.

MARKUS becomes THE DOORMAN.

Librarian 2 There is a knock on the door—Audrey enters.

Librarian 1 She is quiet.

Librarian 3 Poor girl.

Librarian 2 Not sure if she should be there.

Audrey You wanna watch a movie?

Ed Have you been with Simon?…

Audrey Don't ask me that.

Long pause.

Ed You wanna coffee?

Doorman Now we're talking.

ED begins making coffee—the LIBRARIANS begin to help him. There is a chain of help from the ENSEMBLE to hand him the milk and sugar, etcetera, as he struggles to continue a normal conversation.

Ed I'm going to the library—I have to do some reading on Morris West and… Sylvia Plath and… I had this horrible dream… You know? I can't seem to… I've got these things going on in my head. You know?

Audrey Yeah.

Ed The library… All those books and ideas. Gotta be some answers there.

Audrey Yeah.

Ed God. I wish I could kiss you.

Audrey Ed.

Ed I can't help it—

Audrey Why did you say that?!

Ed Because I wanna kiss you, Audrey!

Audrey *You know* I don't want you to say shit like that but you do anyway! That's not love—that's cruelty. It is so fucking selfish!

Ed I am… I am… I am a man who—hurts people.

Audrey What are you talking / about?

Ed None of this comes naturally. /

Audrey Why do you hurt people?!

Ed We need to hurt to know we're alive.

Audrey Do I need to be hurt?

Beat.

Ed Stop.

Audrey I'm asking you a question, Ed.

Ed Please!… I want all this to stop / again!

Audrey You can't just—stop everything.

Ed Why not?! Why not, Audrey? / Stop this now! No!… I don't believe this!

Audrey Answer me, Ed, do I need to be hurt—are you trying to hurt me so you know that you're alive? Is that what this is all / about?!

Ed Audrey… *No! /*

Audrey How do you want me to feel?

39

Bang! Everything stops and ED kisses AUDREY on the mouth.

Jesus—Ed... [*Feeling her lips*] I'm bleeding.

Ed I'm sorry—/ Audrey—please.

Audrey Fuck, Ed—you've fucken...

Ed I'm sorry—

Audrey I can't do this with you. I can't just... let myself kiss you.

Ed Why not? You kiss plenty of other people!

Audrey Not this hard!

Ed Why can't I kiss you, Audrey?!

Audrey Because you can't, / that's it—okay?

Ed Why can't Ed kiss Audrey?!

Audrey Because you mean something to me!

Ed I what?

Audrey This is real—we are... I don't want to destroy us. Listen... I don't *want* you... I *need* you. [*Pause.*] And I miss you, Ed...

Ed I'm right here.

Audrey No you're not. You're not—at all. We used to just—be. Now you're *trying* to *be*—something. Marv's right. You have changed. Ed Kennedy is... better.

    Pause.

Ed And better is bad?

Audrey Better is different. I don't know what to expect anymore. It's not so safe... not so quiet. [*Pause.*] Do you hate me for saying this?

Ed Yes. But I don't blame you.

Audrey Give me a smile.

Ed Don't.

Audrey You can do it.

Ed Audrey—don't.

Audrey I've seen you do it before.

Ed [*smiling weakly*] I feel stupid.

    AUDREY embraces ED.

Audrey Don't. Okay... I want you to know... You know me the best... You treat me the best. When I am with you... I think I feel... like I should.

    A long moment between them.

Markus Okay—this is what we've all been waiting for... Bring in the librarians! I give you... Scene Twenty-Two!

A wonderful flourish of librarian music.

Scene Twenty-Two

The LIBRARIANS bring the books for ED.

Librarian 1 Morris West—
Librarian 2 *Gallows in the Sand—The Clowns of God—The Ringmaster—*
Librarian 3 *Children of the Sun.*
Ed You know me the best and you treat me the best.
Librarian 1 Sylvia Plath!
Librarian 2 'A Winter Ship'—'The Colossus'.
Librarian 3 'Ariel'. 'Crossing the Water' and—
Ed I feel comfortable with you.
Librarian 1 *The Bell Jar.*
Librarian 2 I wanted her titles to be the best.
Librarian 3 So did I.
Ed I think I feel like I should.

He picks up the first book and opens the first page.
A playing card falls out—he picks it up.

The joker. The bloody joker?... Oh, this is a good one. [*Reading*] 'It's simpler than you think.' Right. Simpler than I think... How much more simple can it be than?... I dunno... Okay—obvious and linear narrative—What if the street names are hidden in the book titles? Why not?—'Simpler than you think'... If only I had a street directory....

Librarian music and they present him with a huge street directory.

Librarian 2 The magic of theatre!
Librarian 1 Ready, set...
Librarian 3 Go!
Ed Morris West! Okay—okay—

Racing librarian music as ED flicks through the directory.

Like a game of musical chairs the music screeches to a stop.
ED stops and pats the dog.

Clown Street!
Librarian 3 Good progress! Clown Street!
Librarian 1 And—Sylvia?
Ed Sylvia—right—
Librarian 2 I suggest *The Bell Jar*—
Ed Bell, bell, bell...

Racing librarian music as ED flicks through the books.
The music screeches to a stop.

And—bingo! Bell Street!...
Librarian 3 You're a natural!
Ed Okay—okay—if the titles are the streets—then maybe the chapters are the house numbers?

Racing librarian music as ED flicks through the massive directory—now the action is frenzied.
THE DOORMAN is amused and proud of ED's dedication and then the music screeches to a stop.

Some of these—some of these pages... This number is circled. Twenty-Three Clown Street!

Librarian music fanfare!

Thank you, Morris West!
Librarian 3 Twenty-three Clown Street! A nice place to live!
Ed And... Sylvia Plath—you little ripper! Thirty-nine Bell!

Librarian music fanfare!

Librarian 2 You deserve this, Ed Kennedy.
Librarian 1 The digging is over.
Ed You discovered the code and deciphered the message!
Librarian 1 And you have begun to talk to yourself in the third person.
Ed Is that wrong?
Librarians First step to madness.
Librarian 1 And what a wonderful way to finish the famous... Scene Twenty-Two!

Beat.

Doorman What's next?
Ed Twenty-Three... Clown.

Scene Twenty-Three

Music is playing at Twenty-Three Clown Street—Melusso's Italian Restaurant.

Before our very eyes an Italian restaurant is constructed with CUSTOMERS and WAITERS.

THE DOORMAN becomes MARKUS.

ED is seated at a table and a menu is provided.

The music concludes and ED is watching the DATE—a man in his mid fifties—drinking wine and waiting for a woman. Three WAITERS in balaclavas come to him—all the menus are yellow like the folder.

Ed Why are the waiters wearing balaclavas?
Cyrano [*taking off his balaclava*] Hurry up with all this 'message' shit, will you?! You might have better things to do and as it happens—so do we!
Martin You may not be the only one getting aces in the mail.
Steve Did you ever think of that, smart-arse?
Ed Smart-arse?
Steve Crosses the generations.
Ed Are you going to take my order?
Martin What do you take us for?
Ed Aren't you the waiters?
Steve Only because of you!
Cyrano I recommend the fish.

> *He slaps ED.*

Hurry up.

> *The WAITERS exit and a real WAITRESS arrives.*

Waitress Are you happy sitting here?
Ed Yes.
Waitress How bizarre! Nobody is ever happy sitting at this table. Anyway, it takes all types of crackpots to make an earthenware reject shop. Wine list?! Would you like some wine?!

Ed No thanks. I'll have the spaghetti and meatballs and the lasagne.

Waitress Two main meals? Are you expecting somebody?

Ed No, the lasagne is for my dog—

Waitress You expect our chef to cook lasagne for your dog?!

Ed Yes, I do.

Waitress Where is he?

Ed I'll take it home for him, in a doggie bag.

Waitress Would your dog care to select something from the wine list?

Ed No—he only drinks coffee.

Waitress What a lonely bastard you are. Would you care to see the wine list?

Ed I refuse all drinks at restaurants. I can get a drink anywhere. It's the food that I can't cook—that's what I want. That's what I need.

Waitress When you grow up you will understand. Everything is better when it has the right companion.

> *The WAITRESS leaves in a swirl of accordion and guess who walks through the front door—MA…Beverly Anne Kennedy. ED almost dies and MA makes straight for the DATE.*
>
> *They kiss—as lovers do—and she sits down at the table with the man. They are regulars here—the staff know these two well. They attend to their every need.*
>
> *The food and the wine arrive. ED cannot stand it any longer and walks over to confront the pair. When he arrives, the music and lights snap to nothing.*
>
> *ED and MA are in the spotlight now.*

Ed What are you doing here, Ma?

Ma I have needs, you know?

Ed Needs?

Ma Yes. Now if you don't mind—I would like to resume my dinner date.

Ed Why do you hate me so much?

Ma What?! / What's wrong with you?

Ed You heard me—why do you hate me so much?!

Ma Why do you keep asking?

Ed Because I wanna know!

Ma Well, now is not the time to discuss these things! / I don't wanna make a scene! We have a reputation to consider! Please!

Ed Now is the perfect time—it's the only time! We're already *in* a scene! I have to have an answer from you! Why do you hate me so much?! /

Ma You are as bad as your father! I look at you—and I see his face—your eyes—nose—everything!—and—I hate it. Okay?... You remind me of him.

Ed I love my dad!

Ma Why?... He left nothing for us. I hate to see you following in his footsteps. Now please... I want to eat my meal in peace.

Ed I'm not leaving.

Ma I don't want you here.

Ed You wouldn't treat Tommy this way.

Ma Tommy's not in a crappy Italian restaurant in a crappy bloody town, is he, Ed? Tommy went away to university—he didn't stay home to drive a cab and drink beer on a broken / couch!

Ed That's not fair. /

Ma *Life* isn't fair, Ed—it is something we have to endure!

Ed I am here for you! I haven't vanished, Ma! I am living it with you!

Ma But I don't want you to do that, Ed... We are living in a suburban disaster and your father—he promised me that it would only be temporary... He told me he would get us out of here! 'One day.' 'We'll just pack up and go!'... that's what he said! But look at us... he's gone and we're still here. [*She takes a cigarette and tries to light it.*] You've got potential, Ed. You could be anything—as good as anyone... But not here. If you don't get out now—in forty years time—they will find you on the couch—full of cheap wine and empty promises and that will be a fucking disaster. I don't hate you, Ed... but I cannot stand to see another life getting wasted. I lay awake for my whole married life—waiting for him to stagger home. Where is he now, Ed?... Huh?... Where is he now? [*Pause.*] Save yourself... Get away from me.

Ed I dream of running. In a light blue falcon. It's a beautiful dream like the end of an American movie where the protagonist and his girl drive off into the rest of the world. [*Pause.*] But I drive alone—me and The Doorman. As I sleep—I believe it. Waking up

45

is the shock. I get to my knees at the end of the bed... I don't pray but I come close.

ED takes the unlit cigarette from her mouth.

You look ugly with this in your mouth.

The DATE stands up.

Date You mean—'You look more beautiful, without it'.

Beat—ED looks to DATE and then to MA.

Ed Were you... seeing each other when Dad was alive?

Ma What if I was?

Ed Did Dad know?

Ma He was an alcoholic.

Ed He did his best!

Ma He did nothing of the / sort!

Ed He was a gentleman! /

Ma Nobody said that at his funeral!

Ed Nobody said anything at his funeral.

Ma Exactly!

Ed You should've said something.

Ma Me?

Ed Yeah, what about you, Ma?!

Ma What about *you,* smart-arse?! What about you? Tommy did the reading. Tommy paid for the undertakers. Tommy made sure there were sandwiches for the wake! You sit up the back—and criticise everybody in the distance!

Ed I'm sorry. /

Ma No you're / not!

Ed Yes, I am! /

Ma It's too late. It's too late to be sorry now, Ed.

Pause.

Ed I want stories and songs at my funeral. I want life in the end. We both loved him, Ma... for different reasons... in different times—

Ma But I have *always* loved you. He left us both for dead.

Pause. They embrace for a long time. She kisses him on the face. She pushes the hair from his eyes and looks at him.

You deserve better than me.

She exits and ED and the DATE are face to face.
The DATE gives ED the last ace.

Date This is for you... Ace of hearts.
Ed Four of a kind.
Markus This is Twenty-Four now—

Scene Twenty-Four

Ma Audrey is watching *Cool Hand Luke* at Ed's place.
Markus Marv is on the swing and Ritchie sitting alone at a table in the night.
Ma Ed and The Doorman leave the restaurant.
Mrs Boyd He moves toward Audrey first and then decides to save this for later.
Markus Ed looks at Ritchie and Marv and smiles.
Angelina Ed walks into Ritchie's place—he is listening to talkback radio—late-night callers and races and a few stupid songs.
Markus Eventually Ritchie says—
Ritchie It's waiting for me, Ed. [*Pause.*] Sometimes when I walk home from your place... I think I'm walking, and then I look down at my feet and I realise that I'm going nowhere. It's the world that moves—not me. I don't know how—this happened... You know? How I ended up to be this way. I mean... it's not the robbery. It's not just that. I was born like this—in this place and I have nowhere to go... no idea. I sit in this kitchen every night—listening to the same crap voices... I'm better—I'm stronger... But look at me. I used to wish that I had Chronic Fatigue Syndrome. But I don't... I used to dream of waking up and feeling refreshed and excited. This world is rushing past... I'm staring out the window. You've been following me.
Ed You're on the cards, Ritchie...
Ritchie Me?
Ed Diamonds, clubs, spades and now hearts—this is us. Four of a kind.

Pause.

Ritchie The only thing you're gonna learn from me is how to be a loser, Ed.

Ed No.

Ritchie I'm twenty years old—and... [*Long pause*] I'm twenty years old and there is only one thing in this world that I want.

Ed What is it?

Ritchie I want to want... I want to want something... from this existence. I'm just—here... You know? I'm not—making a difference in anybody's life... Am I?

Ed You make a difference in mine... You do. We need each other.

Ritchie You don't need me.

Ed How do you know what I need?

Ritchie You've got your own place—your own job—you've got it made.

Ed Mate, I drive people around every day, but I'm not going anywhere. They tell me where they have to be and I take them but... I don't have a destination right now... Driving a cab and renting a shack is not going to be the final scene for me. Living like a whisper when they roll the credits?... I don't want this. Do you?

Ritchie No.

Ed Well, there you go—you do want something... Ritchie?

Ritchie What do you want, Ed?

Ed I want friends... but I need love... I want you in my life.

Ritchie Me too.

Ed Well, there you go. That's a start... right?

ED embraces RITCHIE.
RITCHIE looks at ED and then moves away and gently turns the radio off.

Angelina A beautiful silence.

Silence.

Marv I haven't slept in weeks. That bloody robbery... Man... I stare at the ceiling... I know what my priorities are! I am responsible. I have to work... Make money. I pay every fortnight.

MARV and ED eyeball each other.

Ed Did you get your compensation?

48

No response.

Did you get the windscreen fixed?

No response.

So what?… You're driving to work with nothing in front of you?

Marv That's right.

Ed You got forty grand sitting in the bank / and…

Marv Fifty, now.

Ed Fifty thousand dollars?

Marv I work hard, Ed.

Beat.

Ed Okay… What if I need your help, Marv… What if I need some money.

Marv What for?

Ed Does it matter?

Marv I'm not just gonna—give you money.

Ed I thought we were friends?

Marv We are—

Ed You've got fifty grand sitting in the bank doing nothing! But you won't even think about giving / me a loan?

Marv I don't have the money to give / to you!

Ed You just told me that you got fifty grand!

Marv It's spent!

Ed On what?!

Marv On Edgar Street. A term deposit!… The money—is not for me. My life was in that bank and that bastard was tryin' to steal it… with a gun?… in my face?… Suzanne… has a baby… He's two and a half years old. Talk about inciting. A father should provide for his children! Mate… I have a son!… Can you believe it?

Ed It's fantastic!

Marv It's insane.

Ed What does he look like?

Marv I don't know—

Ed Does he look like you?

Marv I don't know, Ed. I've never seen him. [*Pause.*] 'Mr and Mrs Boyd'… Think I ruined their life.

Ed You've saved fifty thousand dollars for a child you haven't even
seen?

Marv Paying off the guilt…

Ed Money isn't going to make you feel better.

Marv What is?

Ed Being there. Go to the house and say, 'I wanna put things right'.

Marv She lives with her parents!

Ed Well, they need to get some perspective!

Marv Me showing up is not going to do that.

Ed I'll come with you. Right by your side.

> *MARKUS becomes THE DOORMAN.*

Marv You'd do that for me?

Ed Nobody can argue with good intention. Where does Suzanne live
now?

Marv Thirty-nine Bell.

Ed How did I know you were going to say that?

Marv I can hear the whole world shaking.

Scene Twenty-Five

*A heartbeat accompanies them as they make their way to the front
door of Suzanne's house.*

ED and THE DOORMAN hang back while MARV walks to the door.

A loud noise of his knuckles on the wood.

*Then MARV is suddenly hurled onto the ground—MR and MRS BOYD
appear at the front door—screaming at MARV.*

Mrs Boyd Get off our property!

Marv Mrs Boyd, I've got fifty thousand dollars!

Mrs Boyd There is a crying child inside this house because of you!
You are not welcome here!

Ed Now how is that helping anybody?!

Mrs Boyd Who on earth are you?!

Ed I'm the guy who's picking up my friend.

Mr Boyd The slug who brought shame upon my family!

Ed Is your grandson a beautiful child?!

Mrs Boyd What?

Ed Your grandson is a human being, sir—is he not beautiful?!

Mr Boyd My grandchild is perfection.

Ed Perfection is not an accident!... It takes two gene pools to do that. His father is here—he wants to repair.

Mr Boyd He's about three years too late!

Ed But he's here, now!

Mr Boyd That means nothing to me!

Ed When you were our age—would you have faced a man like you?

Mr Boyd You're talking gibberish.

Mrs Boyd He is a selfish... fornicator!

Ed Your grandson was born from an act of love.

Mr Boyd How dare you!

Mrs Boyd / No!

Mr Boyd There was no love involved in that / conception!

Mrs Boyd It was sex. Disgusting and demented.

Mr Boyd That's right.

Mrs Boyd We had to leave. Because of him and his filthy seed.

> SUZANNE appears in the doorway.

Ed No. You made that decision. This man is good.

Mrs Boyd Suzie was a child!

Ed They were lovers.

Mrs Boyd He took advantage! /

Mr Boyd He tricked her and he raped her and he hasn't seen her since!

Mrs Boyd That is enough!

Mr Boyd [to SUZANNE] Go back inside! / You shouldn't be seeing this!

Ed He has accumulated a small fortune for this child's future.

Mr Boyd That dirty money's not welcome / in this house!

Mrs Boyd Go away and don't come back!

Ed Why are you deaf to the truth!

Mrs Boyd We know the truth! and we are being punished for this sin!

Ed This isn't about good and evil.

Mrs Boyd *Everything* is about good and evil, boy! We live—we die—we are judged by God. This man committed an act of hatred against my only daughter! Now, I believe that Jesus Christ will save us—but I am prepared to go to Hell and work for the Devil himself, rather than let this demented child molester come near my daughter again!

MR BOYD approaches MARV.

Mr Boyd When you die... You will have to answer for your 'acts of love'. If you want to delay your Day of Rapture... Get off my property now!

MARV stands and eyeballs MR BOYD.

Marv [*quietly*] Liar.
Mrs Boyd Satan! /
Mr Boyd Devil—don't speak to me!
Marv I'm not scared. We both know what happened. I'm not guilty of anything. I am not ashamed of love.

> *Pause.*
> *MARV begins to leave and then...*

The Son of God will stop loving you, if you try to stop me seeing my son.

MARV walks to ED. There is a silence.

MARV touches ED gently on the face and nods.

MARV exits. MR and MRS BOYD go inside.

SUZANNE and ED and MARKUS remain.

Ed You didn't speak in his defence.
Suzanne He hasn't been here.
Ed He didn't know how to find you—you packed up and left!
Suzanne You can't protect him with excuses.
Ed I'm not / protecting him.
Suzanne My father is right.
Ed Did Marvin rape you, Suzanne?
Suzanne He was older and he was careless.
Ed That's not the same thing.
Suzanne If we had stayed—what would my future be?... A teenage mother in a shitty town... Marv was too young... My dad just tried to do the right thing. [*Pause.*] Do you hate me, Ed?... Do you hate me for saying that?

Ed I don't hate anybody. I just feel sorry for all of us—all at once.

Pause.

Suzanne Maybe—you could take me and Markus in your cab one day. Maybe you could drive us somewhere—and maybe Marv might be there waiting. What do you think about that? We could go to a playground—he loves the swings. We could get to know each other... slowly... again...

Ed Okay.

Suzanne Okay.

Ed So tomorrow?...

Suzanne It's a date.

Ed Is that his name?... Markus?

SUZANNE nods.

Marv doesn't know that, does he?

SUZANNE shakes her head.

It's going to be okay.

Suzanne 'Okay'? I don't know what that means anymore, Ed. All I know—it doesn't stop.

THE DOORMAN becomes MARKUS throughout the following.

Ed Life is not just a random series of events, you know? We have some control... Markus... is a strong name. It's a good start... A labour of love.

SUZANNE smiles and exits.
ED and MARKUS are alone.

Markus I am proud of Ed Kennedy.

Ed And I am proud of you.

Markus Me?

Ed Yes... of course.

Pause.

Markus Who do you think I am?

Ed I'd know this ugly bastard anywhere... [*Pause.*] You are the beginning. You are the reason that I... arrive on doorsteps uninvited. I cry and laugh and fight because of you. I have an

53

impact, I am not just another stupid human because of you... We share this journey. You are... you are the doorman to another life. You thought of me. You created me. You will always be my father.

>   *Pause.*

Markus One more to go.
Ed Audrey.
Markus Best till last.
Ed I'm in love with Audrey... right? That's the message, isn't it?
Markus No, Ed... *You* are the message.
Ed Me?
Markus That's the idea.
Ed Okay... So that makes you—the Messenger.

>   *Pause.*

Markus I didn't plan it like that...
Ed No, but it's great. Well done. It was a hoot. Okay. The End.

>   *Worker lights come on—the magic dissolves.*
>   *ED begins to leave MARKUS.*

Markus Where are you going?
Ed I'm going to find Audrey.
Markus Without me?
Ed Yeah...
Markus But I wanna see that bit.
Ed Hey—don't get weird on me, man.
Markus I made her up for you.
Ed And I appreciate it—she is most definitely the best of your creations. But some things—a man's gotta do alone, you know what I'm saying? [*An awkward pause.*] Okay—awkward pause—no more dialogue. Later, dude.
Markus You won't be able to see her without me. She comes from my imagination.
Ed Yes, but I believed you. She exists for me.

>   *AUDREY walks onstage with ED and holds his hand.*
>   *They kiss.*
>   *The ENSEMBLE watch MARKUS watching the two lovers and then...*

54

Goodnight.

They begin to leave him.

Markus Wait! [*Pause.*] Life... is messy.
Ed Like this conclusion. /
Markus Do what I tell ya and you won't get hurt!
Ritchie But we did.
Marv That's the truth.
Markus Please?
Ed What?
Audrey Why are we waiting—I thought this was over?
Markus No.
Angelina What's in your heart, Markus?... What do you really, really want?
Markus I want our last pages to go on forever.
Marv It's time for the playtime to end.
Markus But I have become emotionally involved—in this reality...
Ed And this is when it gets difficult, isn't it?
Markus Real life is more than you can imagine. [*Pause.*] What am I going to do without you?
Audrey Start another story.
Markus You won't be in it.
Ed But it might still be good.
Markus Not as good as this.
Ed I bet that's what you say to all your central characters.
Markus No... just you.
Ensemble You don't need us anymore.
Markus But—I want you in my life.
Audrey We're inseparable—because of you. You give us our breath.

Pause.

Ed If The Doorman was here, he'd just follow me out.
Markus Sometimes I wish I was a dog.

Pause and then we see MARKUS become THE DOORMAN.

ED embraces THE DOORMAN. AUDREY comes and strokes his back.

They hold the image and then... a single playing card falls from the sky.

When it hits the floor of the stage the actors stand and drop all sense of character.

Lights out.

In the darkness playing cards fall onto the audience—they all have messages written on them—sentences from the novel by MARKUS—transcribed by the ENSEMBLE.

THE END

canberra youth theatre presents

THE MESSENGER
THE PLAY
Adapted by Ross Mueller
From the novel by Markus Zusak
Commissioned by Canberra Youth Theatre
Directed by Pip Buining

CAST

Markus/Doorman/Gunman	**Tom Heath**
Ed Kennedy	**Jonathan Sharp**
Marv	**Joshua Bell**
Ritchie	**Matthew Paliaga**
Audrey	**Isobel Nye**
Sophie/Misha/Waitress/Henry	**Megan Johns**
Librarian 1/Police 1/Daryl/Steve/Mrs Boyd	**Tse-Yee Teh**
Librarian 2/Police 2/Hannah/Martin/Mr Boyd	**Katarina Erceg**
Librarian 3/Police 3/Roxanne/	**Emily Goodwin**
Cyrano/Suzanne Boyd	
Woman (Rape Victim)	**Tse-Yee Teh**
Man (Rapist)	**Joshua Bell**
Angelina	**Becky Parkinson**
Ma	**Alison Kelly**
Date	**Andrew Walker**
The Giant	**Ensemble**
Simon	**Ensemble**

PRODUCTION

DIRECTOR/DRAMATURG	**Pip Buining**
WRITER	**Ross Mueller**
DESIGNER	**Tobhiyah Feller**
SOUND DESIGNER	**Kimmo Vennonen**
LIGHTING DESIGNER	**Mark Gordon**
SINGER/SONGWRITER	**Andrew Walker**
ASSISTANT DIRECTOR	**Anne Marie Serrano**
PRODUCTION MANAGER	**Sue Webeck**
STAGE MANAGER	**Alana Teasdale**
FRONT OF HOUSE	**Jo Michajlow**
TECHNICAL MANAGER	**Anthony Arblaster**
SOUND OPERATOR	**Michael Foley**
SET CONSTRUCTION	**Sudzset**
SCENIC ART ASSISTANT	**Nicola Lohan**
SEAMSTRESS	**Victoria Worley**
PHOTOGRAPHER	**'pling**
DESIGN	**DesignEdge**

CANBERRA YOUTH THEATRE

ARTISTIC DIRECTOR	**Pip Buining**
GENERAL MANAGER	**Sharon Casey**
PART-TIME WORKSHOP COORDINATOR	**Adam Hadley**

MANAGEMENT COMMITTEE:

Caroline Fulton (President), Mark Gordon (Vice President), Estelle Muspratt, Michael Hennessey, Kristil-Rae Mobbs, Stephen Barker, Anne Quinn, Sue Webeck, Rosalin Mawlanazada

Canberra Youth Theatre (CYT) was established in 1972 and is the longest established youth theatre in Australia. CYT is a nationally recognised youth arts company which creates and promotes theatre with young people that is inspirational, enriching, collaborative and innovative.

CYT provides young people ages 7-25 with the opportunity to explore, extend and develop their creativity through theatre workshops and productions. We create theatre that encourages participants to voice their ideas and promote their experience of the world. CYT has a history of successfully commissioning work, the most well known of which is *Dags* by Debra Oswald. CYT is committed to supporting emerging artists; our young people work with professional artists, unleashing their imaginations in order to create engaging and challenging theatre. www.cytc.net

The adaptation of The Messenger was made possible through the generous support of Paperchain Bookstore and The Rock Development Group whilst the CYT Actors Ensemble is proudly supported by Canberra Milk.

Canberra Youth Theatre is proudly supported by its members, the ACT government through artsACT and the ACT Health Promotions Grant Program, and the Australian Government through the Australia Council, its arts funding and advisory body.

DIRECTOR'S NOTES: PIP BUINING

I would like to begin with my thank yous because if Markus had never written the book then I wouldn't have commissioned Ross to adapt it and I would not be writing these notes. So... thank you Markus for creating *The Messenger* and for so freely entrusting us with the adaptation and thank you Ross for joyfully and open heartedly embarking on the adaptation journey with me. Thank you also to my wonderful creative and production teams and thank you to the CYT Actors Ensemble for your commitment, passion and good humour – it has been a joy to work with you.

Thanks also to the three local Canberra businesses who were moved by *The Messenger*. Canberra Milk, The Rock Development Group and Paperchain Bookstore's generous support has enabled young people to actively engage with their local community through the arts.

The Messenger provided opportunities for emerging writers, performers and technicians to observe and actively engage with the adaptation process. The project allowed these young artists to learn from, and work alongside, professional theatre makers and to work with a script that they could relate to and creatively engage with.

The adaptation of *The Messenger* began in 2006 when I accepted the position of Artistic Director at CYT. At that time the participants of CYT had expressed a desire for us to commission a playwright to adapt a contemporary Australian work of fiction for them to perform. And so, with their assistance, I compiled a list of books and began to read - young adult fiction piled up next to my bed ... one story wanted to be retold, *The Messenger* resonated with us all.

Set inside the authors mind we find ourselves in the depths of a suburban disaster, we are unknowingly passive, but as the clock ticks we all begin to wish for something more ... *The Messenger* is a darkly humorous, thought provoking and moving story that reminds us how difficult it is for some young people to find their place in the world. It doesn't promise that "everything will be ok" – but there is hope and there is a place in the world for Ed Kennedy. *The Messenger* is a timely narrative about engagement. In a climate of self-preservation and self-absorption this story provides hope. It is a story for our community, all communities. As Ed himself states:

> Christ, it's deafening. Why can't the world hear? I ask myself. Within a few moments I ask it many times. Because it doesn't care, I finally answer, and I know I'm right. It's like I have been chosen. But chosen for what? I ask. The answer's quite simple: to care.

from *The Messenger* by Markus Zusak

PLAYWRIGHT'S NOTES: ROSS MUELLER

A book is always going to be different to the film or the song or the play. A book can take time and ruminate and whisper, good theatre can do this too — but in the end good theatre is constructed from action in time and space. It is always in the present tense for the audience. It is always happening right now — tonight — in front of our very eyes. We, the audience, are reading the action of the play at the same time, we are not getting up for cups of tea and snatching a few minutes on the train to work. The action on stage is the only evidence that we have — we cannot flick back and check up on stuff we've missed or forgotten. Therefore when we began the process of adaptation we were looking for the true action in the book.

Left to right : Tom Heath and Joshua Bell in rehearsal. Photo by 'pling

Ed Kennedy is a pretty lethargic character, he lets life happen to him, but the key dramatic action in the book is when Ed physically confronts the bank robber and then the rapist. These two actions are in the first quarter of the book. It is from these confrontations, that Ed feels a confidence and compulsion to go forward and see the world in a way that he has never gazed before. Pip and I agreed early on that these scenes were key for the book to become a stage play. From here our task was to identify the message of *The Messenger* and squeeze about four hundred pages into about ninety minutes.

An author has a potentially never ending cast — but a playwright faces the reality that some poetry is going to be limited by the numbers of bodies available. This truth is a challenge and an opportunity. It demands that decisions are made, that scenes and chapters are deleted or merged and some voices silenced and some voices amplified. Markus was great about this. Early on in the process he had given email instruction to do whatever we wanted. This freedom of expression allowed us to concentrate on making a piece of theatre, rather than chronicling an already beautifully written novel.

As Pip and I worked, we realised (very early on) that Markus was indeed a key character. His voice was echoing throughout the chapters and therefore he must be a presence on stage. Once this decision had been taken, we were able to make bold choices like giving The Doorman a real voice. This was an exciting decision.

A talking dog is automatically accepted in theatre. In literature it is another story altogether. We see him and hear him so we believe him and his words can be more than just dialogue. The

Doorman embodies the soul of *The Messenger*. He is our access to Zusak. His thoughts are his dialogue and as a character — for an actor — The Doorman is truly a theatrical gift.

Another element in the task of adaptation was fitting the story into the physical space. I was very lucky to be able to see the space before I began my writing task. CYT flew me up to see the theatre and so I knew my environment like an author might research a suburb. Meeting the cast was the final essential in the process for me. A good playwright writes for actors and so when you can see and hear the actors you will be working for, you write with conviction. It has been a great eighteen months living and working with Ed and The Doorman and the Librarians and the Boyd family and all of the people that exist in our minds — on the stage — when we see the play — of the book — if you know what I mean.

I want to thank Markus Zusak for writing *The Messenger* and for entrusting me with the role of introducing it to the stage. It was a pleasure and a privilege to work with the amazing Pip and her terrific team at CYT on this adaptation of *The Messenger*.

Left to right: Tse-Yee Teh, Emily Goodwin, Katarina Erceg, Jonathan Sharp, Megan Johns, Alison Kelly, Joshua Bell, Isobel Nye in rehearsal. Photo by 'pling

AUTHOR'S NOTES: MARKUS ZUSAK

I was eating fish and chips in a park in Kiama.

There was a bank on the other side of the road.

Outside the bank, there was a fifteen minute parking zone, and I thought, 'Fifteen minutes? Every time I go into the bank there's a frighteningly long queue. There's a painfully slow cashier. There are kids going berserk at the Lego table, or scribbling all over the deposit slips ... No, fifteen minutes is nowhere near long enough.'

From there, I thought, 'What if you were in that bank while it was getting robbed and your car was out there? How would you get out to move your car and avoid getting a fine?'

A few days later I wrote the first chapter of *The Messenger*. Ed Kennedy and his three hapless friends were face down on the floor, the robbery was a farce, and one of Ed's mates was yelling at the gunman to hurry up. I didn't know what would happen next. I didn't know that Ed would become a messenger or a message.

In the end, I'm grateful for the idea that fell into my lap in Kiama. I love that one idea spirals into another, and then you can see it all on stage, with new vision, new minds, and young people who are also pursuing ideas in their own ways.

Lastly, I have to be realistic. At the time of writing this, *The Messenger* was released six years ago. Experience has shown me that I buggered up the ending, although it's something I don't regret. Now I take solace in the fact that I was willing to take a risk, which led me to better work in my next book. That, and I thank Ross Mueller for fixing it in his adaptation. I'm also grateful to Ross, Pip Buining and CYT for achieving more than I could have hoped for in their own version of *The Messenger*. They've managed to keep its essence and make it new.

"If it's one thing that I'm going to take away from working on The Messenger, and with the CYT Actors Ensemble, it's that we can all make a difference in someone else's life. All we have to do is care. This project has made me realise that truth, and encouraged me to put it to use. I've begun to look deeper at the lives of my friends and family, to look beyond the masks that we all wear, and be there for those of them who are crying out for help. It's been wonderful working with such a great group of people, and I'll definitely miss the ability to suddenly transform into a dog!"

Tom Heath, 2008 CYT Actors Ensemble

Above: front: Jonathan Sharp, Tom Heath; background: Emily Goodwin, Katarina Erceg, Tse-Yee Teh, Joshua Bell, Becky Parkinson, Megan Johns, Andrew Walker
Facing page: left to right: Emily Goodwin, Tse-Yee Teh, Katarina Erceg. Joshua Bell
Photos by 'pling

ROSS MUELLER
PLAYWRIGHT

Ross Mueller is a multi-award winning playwright. His latest play, *Concussion*, was showcased at the 2008 National Play Festival, was shortlisted for the Patrick White Award and Griffin Award and won the 2008 New York Dramatists Award. The Glory won the 2007 Wal Cherry Play of the Year and premiered at Hothouse Theatre Company. Ross's play *The Ghost Writer* premiered at the Melbourne Theatre Company in 2007 and has since been produced in Brisbane and Perth and Construction of the Human Heart was shortlisted for the New York New Dramatists Award and was shortlisted for the 2007 AWGIE Award for Best New Play. First produced by The Storeroom, *Construction* was then presented at the Malthouse and toured the eastern states. In 2007 *No Man's Island* had its US premiere at Here in New York City. In 2002 Ross was the Australian playwright at the International Residency of the Royal Court Theatre in London. Ross has been commissioned by Playbox, Melbourne Theatre Company, Hothouse and ABC Radio National. He has been an affiliate of the Melbourne Theatre Company, a founding member of Melbourne Dramatists and a number of his plays are published. His other works include; *A Party in Fitzroy, Little Brother, Great Ocean Road, Colosseum, Pinters Explanation* and (A pilot version of...) *Something To Die For*. Most recently, Ross has written the text for the contemporary performance piece *Appetite*, being presented at the Melbourne International Arts Festival.

MARKUS ZUSAK
AUTHOR

Markus Zusak was born in 1975 and is the author of five books, including the international bestseller, *The Book Thief*. His first three books, *The Underdog, Fighting Ruben Wolfe* and *When Dogs Cry*, released between 1999 and 2001, were all published internationally and garnered a number of awards in Australia. *The Messenger*, published in 2002, won the 2003 CBC Book of the Year Award (Older Readers) and the 2003 NSW Premier's Literary Award (Ethel Turner Prize), as well as receiving a Printz Honour in America. In 2005, *The Book Thief* was released and is now translated into thirty languages. As well as receiving awards in Australia and overseas, *The Book Thief* has held the number one position at Amazon.com, Amazon.co.uk and the *New York Times* bestseller list. It also reached the number one spot in Brazil, Ireland and Taiwan. It has been in the top five in the UK, Spain, Norway, Israel and Korea. The Age calls it 'an original, moving, beautifully written book'. The Guardian: 'A novel of breathtaking scope, masterfully told'. The *New York Times*: 'Brilliant and hugely ambitious...the kind of book that can be life-changing'. Markus lives in Sydney with his wife and daughter.

Awards for The Messenger
2006 Michael L Printz Award Honor book
2006 Bulletin Blue Ribbon Book
2005 Publishers Weekly Best Books of the
        Year — Children
2003 Children's Book Council of Australia Book of
        the Year Award

PIP BUINING
DIRECTOR/DRAMATURG

Pip Buining is the Artistic Director of Canberra Youth Theatre (2006-) and has worked with young performing artists since 1994. Over the last 15 years she has worked professionally as a Dramaturg, Director, Event Coordinator and Teacher, including several years freelance at Sydney Theatre Company, three years Directing at a performing arts high school, sessional lecturing at Sydney University and ACU, event coordinating for the Australia Day Celebrations in Sydney and a casual stint teaching in a Juvenile Justice Centre. She has run innumerable theatre workshops and directed productions in a variety of contexts. She has a Bachelor of Education (University of Sydney), MA in Theatre Studies (University of NSW) and Certificate in Film Production (New York University). She is currently developing TANK, sustainable touring theatre located inside a portable theatrical water tank, and a performance installation to be performed at the National Library entitled *Retrieval*.

TOBHIYAH FELLER
DESIGNER

Tobhiyah Feller is a proud member of the CYT alumni beginning her career as the first participant in the 'Engagements' program at CYT in 2000 while in year 12 at Narrabundah College. She moved to Sydney when she finished school to study Sculpture at COFA (College of Fine Arts UNSW). She has since completed a Bachelor of Dramatic Arts in Design at NIDA and now works professionally as a production designer. Her professional design credits include: Set Design *Wilde Tales* (State of Play); Set and Costume Design *A View of Concrete* (B Sharp); *Camarilla* (Merrigong Theatre Company); *Words Are Weapons* and *Battlegrounds* (ATYP); *This Territory* (ATYP/PYT); *Les Miserables* (Alexander Productions); *Burn, The Miracle* and *Fugee* (NSW Public Schools' Drama Co.); *Last of The Knucklemen* (Brand X) and *Human Resources* (Siren Theatre Co.). Tobhiyah is delighted to have this opportunity to return to CYT and offer her skills in design to the company.

KIMMO VENNONEN
SOUND DESIGNER

Kimmo Vennonen is involved in many activities combining music and electronics. He can usually be found at his CD mastering and music production studio in Gorman House Arts Centre. He is also Treasurer and engineer at Community Radio 2XX, following a period as station manager in 2005 and 2006. He has worked as a freelance sound recordist, with Canberra theatre companies as sound designer, played with prominent Sydney improvising musicians and put together interactive sound installations. He has been an ANU Visiting Fellow and is privately researching three dimensional sound. Specialising in music mastering and sound design, he has a diverse base of clients in the arts, from Canberra and beyond...

MARK GORDON
LIGHTING DESIGNER

Mark Gordon graduated from Rusden State College (now Deakin University) with a Bachelor of Education majoring in Drama, Dance and Media Studies. He worked freelance as a dancer, choreographer, stage manager, theatre technician and taught in tertiary institutions for many years. His has worked for: Tasdance, Ausdance Victoria, The National Theatre Drama School and Ballet School, The Australian Choreographic Centre and the Department of the Environment, Water, Heritage and the Arts. He served on the ACT Cultural Council and as guest peer for the Australia Council. In 2001 he was awarded The Centenary of Federation Medal for 'service to society and choreography' and in 2006 the Australian Dance Award for 'Services to dance'. Mark has designed lighting for dance and theatre productions since 1975.